# SCHIRMER'S LIBRARY
OF MUSICAL CLASSICS

Vol. 378

CARL CZERNY

Op. 261

Exercises in Passage-Playing

One Hundred and Twenty-Five
Elementary Studies for the Piano

Edited and Fingered by

G. BUONAMICI

G. SCHIRMER, *Inc.*

DISTRIBUTED BY

7777 W. BLUEMOUND RD. P.O. BOX 13819 MILWAUKEE, WI 53213

125
Exercises in Passage-playing.

Repeat each Exercise several times.

Allegro.

C. CZERNY. Op. 261, Book I.

*) It is excellent practice to play the first 10 exercises in C♯ as well, using the same fingering wherever practicable.

Allegro.

5.

Allegro.

6.

Allegretto vivace.

7.

p leggermente.

cresc.

6

Allegro moderato.

14.

15.

Allegretto.

Allegretto.

16.

*) Also transpose into G♭.

8

18.

Allegro vivo.

*)

Allegro.

19.

*) Also transpose into D♭.

Allegretto vivace.

22.

14

Allegro vivace.

33.

Allegro moderato.

34.

Andante.

35.

*) Also transpose a semitone higher.

*) Also transpose into F♯, using the same fingering.

125
Exercises in Passage - playing.

Allegro moderato.

C. CZERNY. Op. 261, Book II.

*) Also practise in B major.   **) Perform the trill thus:

125
Exercises in Passage-playing.

Allegro scherzoso.

C. CZERNY. Op. 261, Book III.

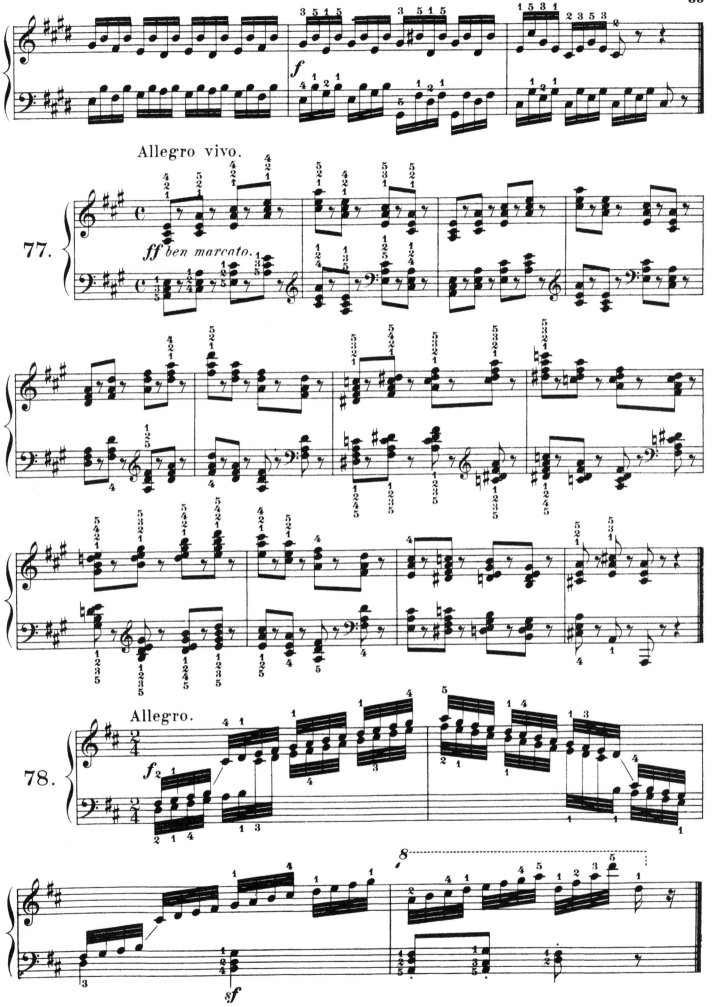

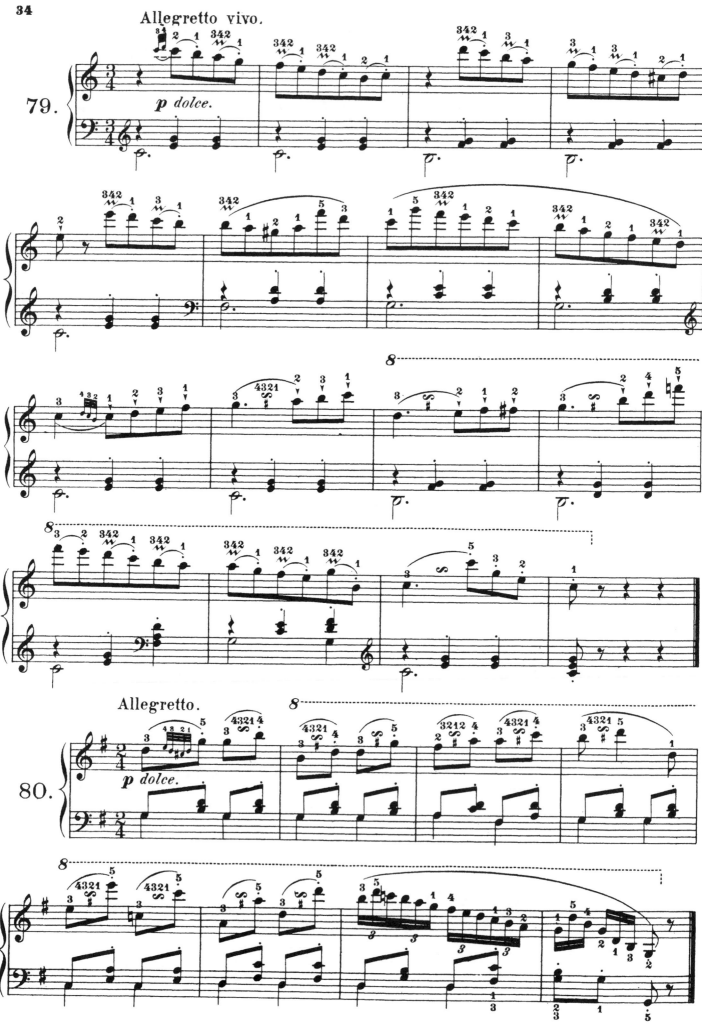

Allegretto.

87.

Allegro.

88.

*) Also practise in D♭.

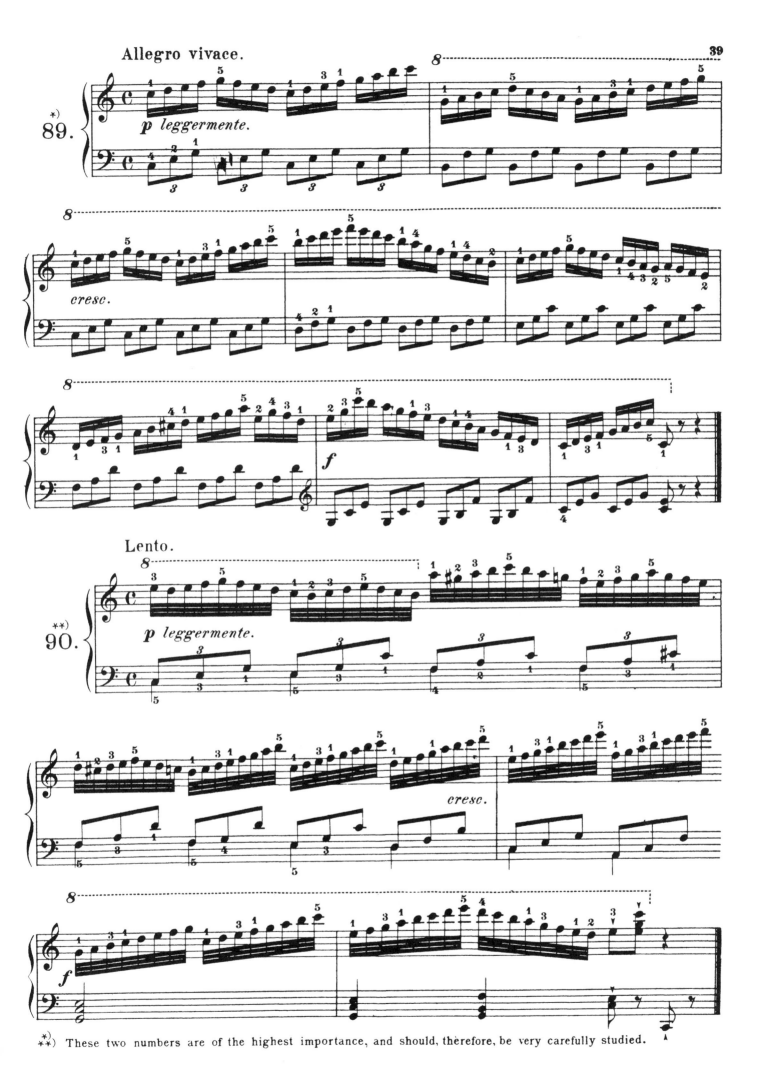

*) \
**) These two numbers are of the highest importance, and should, therefore, be very carefully studied.

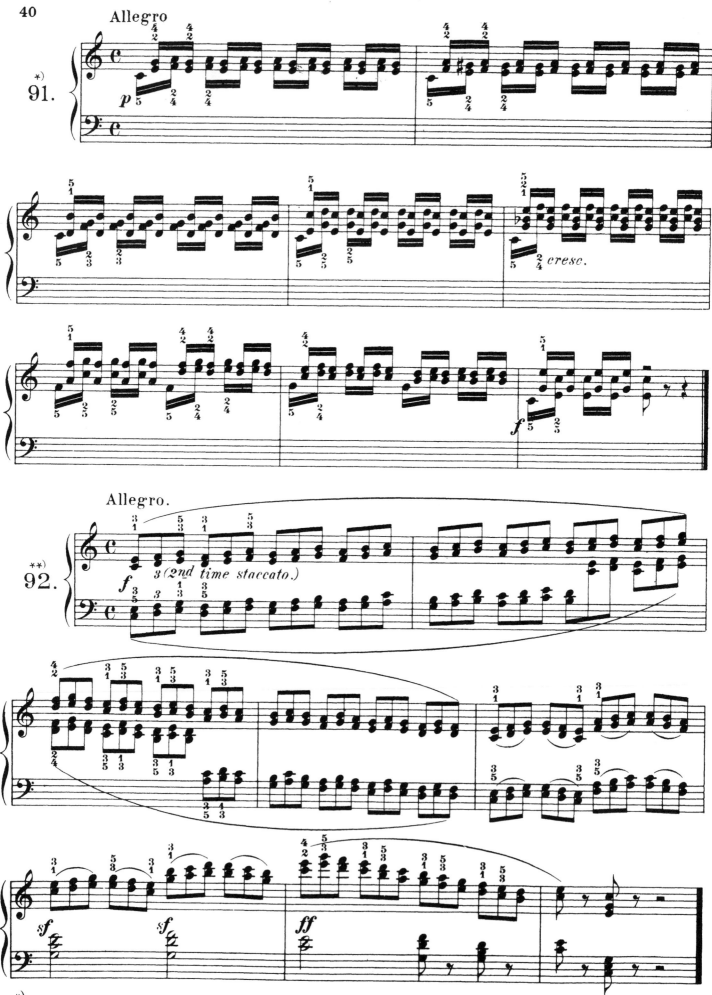

40

Allegro

91.

Allegro.

92.

*) Also transpose a semitone higher.

Allegro molto.

95.

Allegretto.

96.*)

*) Also transpose into B-major.

Perform the trill thus:
etc.

Allegro molto vivo.

Allegro.

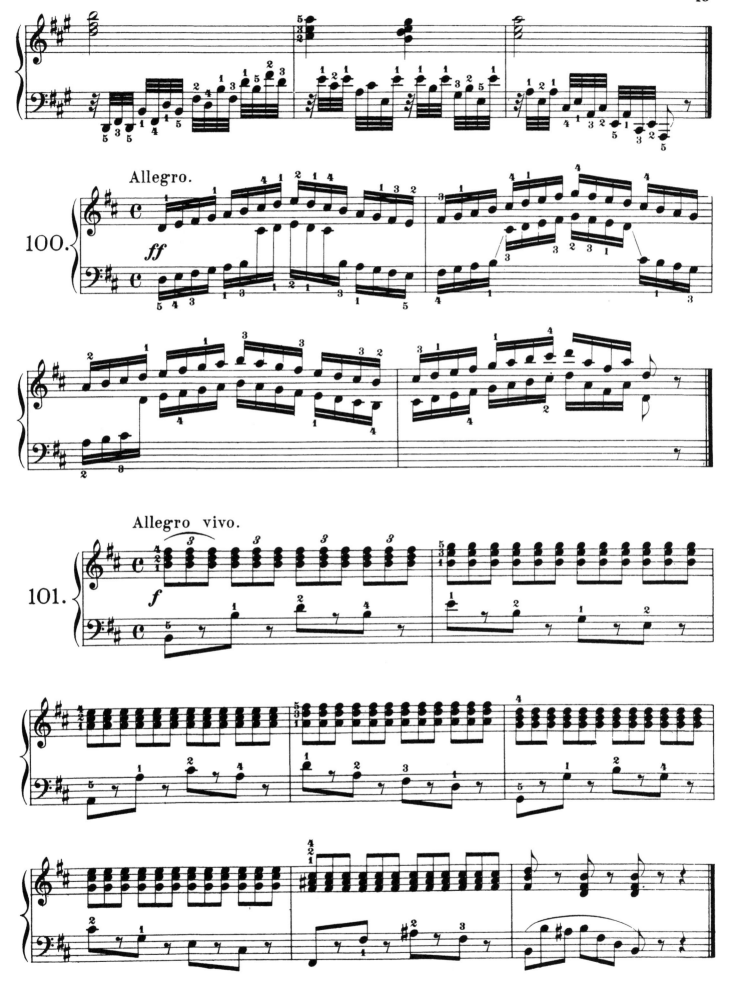

125
Exercises in Passage-playing.

C. CZERNY. Op. 261. Book IV.

Allegro vivace e scherzando.

104.

p dolce e leggero

111.

Allegro vivo.

Moderato e mesto.

115.

Allegro moderato.

116.

Allegretto animato.

117.

Allegro molto vivace.

118.

Andante espressivo e cantabile.

119.

*) Also practise in B-minor.

*) Also transpose a semitone lower.